THE RENEWED MIND

A Collection of Teachings by
Dr. Victor Paul Wierwille

Transcribed and Edited by
Rev. Rocky T. Sanders

Matthew 5:9 Blessed are the peacemakers: for they shall be called the
children of God.

DEDICATION

This work is dedicated to my wife who has continued to support me in all my endeavors. She is the light of my life and my companion in all things. And she still looks good at 60 something.

INDEX

INTRODUCTION

When I began writing on the renewed mind I wanted to give the reader a better understanding of how to apply God's word in their life according to Romans 12:2. In researching the subject matter, I discovered that much of it had already been covered many decades' past by another man of God, Dr. Victor Paul Wierwille. However; what he had presented was in verbal form, so I began transcribing his teachings. And what I saw was that by compiling those teachings in booklet form would make available to the masses the inherent accuracy of God's word pertaining to this subject.

I have attempted to be as accurate as possible in my transcriptions. However, I found that I needed to edit certain portions of the original spoken teachings so they would fit in written form.

There are many areas in the word of God that we need to renew our minds to; health, prosperity, faithfulness, prayer, understanding, sharing, fellowship, and many others. Dr. Wierwille taught us that the renewed mind is the key to power in our individual walk with God.

In his book, *"Power for Abundant Living"* he wrote:

> "What does it mean to "renew one's mind"? It means "to hold The Word in mind and act accordingly." The Greek word for the renewed mind is literally translated "transfigured" or "transformed," *metamorphoó*. Believers are to get a new form, a new figure in mind."

We will learn many new and informative things from the teachings recorded here. But the most important thing I want everyone to take away from reading this booklet is that "if you walk by the revealed Word of God, you will manifest the greatness of the power of God." Dr. Victor Paul Wierwille, "*Power for Abundant Living*", ©1971.

PART ONE

1 CORINTHIANS 13, PRACTICING THE RENEWED MIND

SNT 0841
December 26, 1976

Take your bibles tonight, please, and go to 1 Corinthians.

Because of the ministry, and the things we helped people with this week. More and more this chapter in Corinthians became a realty in my heart to the end that I thought I ought to share it again tonight. For many of you in the Way Ministry it's an old chapter. A chapter that you have read time and time again. And as I look across the ministry and around the world I wonder if we could not learn this chapter, in action, even better.

There's a record about a King in Africa who was not a Christian. But he invited a Christian to come to him and to read to him because he had heard that the bible was a good book to read. So he read to him from the third chapter of James that section about the tongue being an unruly evil full of deadly poisons therewith bless we God, therewith curse we men. And he read him that wonderful section, and before he left he told the missionary who read it, he said, whenever I want you to read again I'll call you. So the missionary waited a week and the King didn't call. Waited two weeks and he didn't call. Waited 52 weeks and he didn't call. So finally he just couldn't stand it any longer, and he went back to the court and he asked for permission to speak to the King. And he said to the King when he met with him, how come you never invited me back, did I insult you, what did I say that could have hurt you? He said, it isn't in what you said, I just haven't learned the lesson yet. That's why I didn't invite you back.

So, it's just not a knowledge of the word in the head, it's putting it into practice, learning it. 1 Corinthians 13 is like that. Sandwiched between the great twelfth and fourteenth chapters of Corinthians sits probably the greatest chapter in the whole word of God. When it comes to putting into practice the greatness of the new birth. Living the mystery in a practical way. I think of course the 12th chapter is fantastic, the 14th chapter is great. But I think the 13th chapter is sandwiched in between that if it were put any other place in the bible you would lose its great dynamic impact.

Perhaps before we read this chapter, and we're going to go through it line by line I ought to define for you the word charity. You'll see the word charity in the first verse of the 13th chapter.

Whenever we think, as Americans today, about the word charity, we think about the Red Cross or the Salvation Army. And, you know, if you have a little bit of a catastrophe we come in with a cup of coffee, clothing and a few other things. That's not the word charity. The word charity is the word *agapeo* which is love, the word love. And when I first gathered the greatness of this word and its usage in the word (of God) the 13th chapter fit for me. Until that time it did not fit. Perhaps the reason I got it to fit is because I always thought of love as being a gift of God to me, which it is. But this word agapeo as charity is not God's gift to me, it is my putting on, up here in my mind what God has given to me. It's the love of God transferred from the inner man, which is

6

Christ in you the hope of glory, from the inner man to your mind. It's putting on the mind of Christ, it is let this mind be in you which was in Christ Jesus, put ye on the lord Jesus Christ. This is that love.

Maybe before we read the 13th chapter we outa read Colossians. In chapter 3 of Colossians there is this great 14th verse.

Colossians 3:14
And above all these things *put on* charity, which is the bond of perfectness.

The word bond is the cohesiveness, that which binds things together. Like you cement together two pieces of broken glass, that's bonding it together. Or you put together two pieces of drywall, that's bonding material.

So if you want to have that cohesiveness which is perfectness you have to put on charity. And charity is *agapeo*. Whatever God gives to me as a gift I don't put on. Whatever I put on is works. When I got dressed today that was works. What God does in Christ in you is grace, what you do is works. It says put on, what you put on that's works. Therefore, charity, that you put on, is the love of God in the renewed mind in manifestation because you put it on. God gave it to you in Christ Jesus. When you were born again of God's spirit, that love of God is in you because it is Christ in you the hope of glory. You've got it inside you, but having it inside you doesn't help you until you get it up in your mind. It helps you as far as eternal life is concerned, sure. You are heaven bound and all hell can't stop you if you have it inside you. But until you get it on in your mind you still live in defeat and lies. You're still negative and all the rest of the junk that is the natural man.

Now that love of God is that manifestation of the evidence of Christ in your mind. Where you renew your mind and you evidence it, you manifest that love of God. That's the word charity. And it should always be translated: the love of God in the renewed mind in manifestation. If you translated it that way, you'll have the truth of God's word and it will fit like a hand in a glove.

Now let's look at that great 13th chapter of 1 Corinthians, and let's begin with verse 1.

1 Corinthians 13:1
Though I speak with the tongues of men and of angels, and have not charity *(the love of God in the renewed mind in manifestation)*, I am become *as* sounding brass, or a tinkling cymbal.

You will notice that this 1st verse is contingent upon the 31st verse of the previous chapter where it says to covet earnestly, earnestly desire, the best gifts. And yet, he says, I show you a more excellent way. A more excellent way than what? Than earnestly desiring it. And that excellent way is the love of God in the renewed mind in manifestation.

You put on the love of God in the renewed mind in manifestation people, and there's nothing else you have to ask God for, it will be there. You never have to ask; it will always be there.

All speaking in tongues is speaking with the tongues of men or of angels. You will either speak with a tongue that is known upon the earth, or a tongue that angels converse in.

8

Don't ask me what it's all about because I've never been an angel. You see, even though I would speak with the tongue of men or angels, and be tremendous like in a believers meeting. Whenever someone comes in and says, "oh, isn't reverend Rocky terrific. He speaks in tongues, he interprets, he's just dynamite." It doesn't amount to one lousy thing, it doesn't mean a thing, and I don't have the charity, don't have the love of God in the renewed mind in manifestation, I am become as sounding brass or a tinkling cymbal. Nothing wrong with the speaking in tongues and interpretation, there is something wrong with me.

I am become...*I* am become...*I* am become...as sounding brass of a tinkling cymbal.

Am I saved? Sure! Am I going to heaven? Yes, no hell can stop me. But I'm just not living like I ought to be living. Not manifesting in the greatness of the power of God. That's why the love of God in the renewed mind in manifestation is the greatest thing we have to have in the Way Ministry. You can be so right on God's word and be so adamant about it and rightly divide it and do everything else but it you haven't got the love of God in your heart, real love for people, you might as well chuck everything. You'll be as sounding brass, or a tinkling cymbal. Then life will be totally miserable for you and everybody else you come in contact with. You make them miserable too. You see, you're always dogging them; why don't you believe God's word, why don't you get onto God's word, why don't you turn to God's word, why don't you get saved. Oh hell, who wants to get saved, not me. I wouldn't want to get saved either if somebody laid that on me. You know why, no love. The love of God in the renewed mind is the greatest healing thing in the whole world. And somewhere in the word it says that that kind of love covers a whole multitude of sins. Otherwise, without the love of God in the renewed mind it's just going through the act.

That's why this 13th chapter cries like tears today again among God's people. Because people are not living this 13th chapter. It's just a head trip, it's a mental assent. It's a nice thing, it's in the word of God, it's beautiful to read, makes me feel nice and peaceful come Christmas time. I was thinking about the holy land. The holy land is the most un-holiest place in the world. They talk about peace over there but they fight like crazy. What a bunch of crap, it's bologna. You have to be an adult to understand it. A 5-year-old child would regurgitate on it, they'd say that is no good, that's counterfeit, that's a bunch of bologna. You've got to be an adult to grow out of that honesty, and put up with that junk. And that's exactly what's happening with so called Christians, they are just putting up with it. Well some of us are tired of putting up with it. Let's get back to the word and let this word of God live dynamically.

Nothing wrong with speaking in tongues and interpretation; something wrong with me. Because I am become as sounding brass, or a tinkling cymbal if I don't have the   love   of God in the renewed mind in manifestation. Verse 2 says.

1 Corinthians 13:2
And though I have *the gift of* prophecy, and understand all mysteries, and all knowledge; and though I have all faith, so that I could remove mountains, and have not charity, I am nothing.

"The gift of" is in italics so scratch it because prophecy is a manifestation, not a gift. And though I have prophecy, in other words if I could prophesy. And understand all mysteries, that is the great mystery that was kept hidden since the world began, that the gentiles should be fellow heirs and of the same body. And have all knowledge regarding that mystery and the word. And though I have all faith, the word faith is the word *pistis*. The word *pistis* here should be translated believing. Though I have all believing so that I could remove mountains. And have not, the word and here should be the word but. But have not charity, the love of God in the renewed mind in manifestation, I am nothing. That's what the word says, that's what it means. I am nothing.

If I had all believing that I could remove mountains. That's pretty interesting that statement, because if you go to Mark 11

Mark 11:21-23
[21] And Peter calling to remembrance saith unto him, Master, behold, the fig tree which thou cursedst is withered away.

[22] And Jesus answering saith unto them, Have faith (*pistis, believing*) in God.

[23] For verily I say unto you, That whosoever shall say unto this mountain, Be thou removed, and be thou cast into the sea; and shall not doubt in his heart, but shall believe that those things which he saith shall come to pass; he shall have whatsoever he saith.

Whosoever in verse 23 means just that, whosoever. Christian or non-Christian, Jew or Gentile, whosoever. And shall not doubt in his heart but believe, *pistis*, he'll get whatsoever he says. That's what Corinthians is talking about. And though I have all believing so I can say to that mountain go jump in the lake, literally. The reason you can't tell that mountain to go jump in the lake is because you doubt it to begin with. You believe it, you say to it and God will do it. But you see, man is so smart in the head, that he's doubting all the time. Man's a real genius isn't he! He knows all the time that God isn't going to do anything so naturally what's God going to do, nothing. He already knows He can't do anything. You get exactly what you believe for.

This mountain, or the removal of this mountain in Corinthians, is contingent on that greatness of that revelation in Mark. Say to this mountain, be removed, cast into the sea, and shall not doubt but believe what he says will come to pass and he will get whatsoever he says. This is why, many times, the unbelievers get many more answers than the believers because the unbelievers just believe when they say something it's going to happen. But a believer gets so religious that he gets condemned about being so religious. You know he doesn't pray 50 hours a day, or something like that, he feels God's not going to do anything. Answers to prayer are not contingent upon how many hours you spend praying, it is contingent upon your believing. The reason people have to pray so long is because they believe so little usually.

In Matthew is another record we need to look at.

Matthew 17:19-20
[19] Then came the disciples to Jesus apart, and said, Why could not we cast him out?

[20] And Jesus said unto them, Because of your unbelief: for verily I say unto you, If ye have faith *(pistis, believing)* as a

grain of mustard seed, ye shall say unto this mountain, Remove hence to yonder place; and it shall remove; and nothing shall be impossible unto you.

This verse is often mis-quoted. Some say, "it you have faith the size of a grain of mustard seed." Size doesn't matter. It doesn't say the size of a grain of mustard seed. It says believing, *pistis*, as a grain of mustard seed. Because the power that's latent in the smallest seed will crack the hardest granite. Some of you who have traveled in mountain areas have seen a small tree that is growing right out of the rock. Split that rock wide open. It isn't the size of the seed, it's to life that's in it. If you have believing as a grain of mustard seed, not size, but have that believing, that life, that dynamic there, you can say to that mountain be removed to the sea, and it will be as you say.

You see people, it that isn't God's word then what is God's word. If you can throw out those scriptures than you can throw out John 3:16. You can throw out anything you want. It's either God's word or it isn't God's word. Now just because something comes to pass or doesn't come to pass does not substantiate it or invalidate it. The truth is God's word. Whether or not I believe it is not the criteria. It's still God's word whether I believe it or I don't believe it. The word says if you doubt it's never going to come to pass. It's in the believing of it. And that believing is the love of God in the renewed mind. That's the greatest thing. I was thinking if we could end this year with the love of God in the renewed mind and launch into the next year with that believing, wouldn't that be the greatest thing!

Now verse three, it's a good one.

1 Corinthians 13:3
And though I bestow all my goods to feed *the poor*, and though I give my body to be burned, and have not charity, it profiteth me nothing.

The poor, even though it is in italics, it is well supplied here. It means those that are less fortunate. If I had 10 million dollars and gave all that money to build something for the poor I bet every newspaper and TV station in the region would come down and do a story on it. If I gave it away on Christmas, wouldn't that be wonderful.

If I bestow **allllll**... my goods to feed the poor, and even if I gave my body to be burned; which simply means that I dedicated myself to those gifts that I gave and say from now on I will work only for Social Services or the new hospital in town, but have not the love of God in the renewed mind it profits me nothing. Would it profit a lot of other people? Oh sure! And there's the great key. The true God never puts it on a basis of just profiting others. Every time you do anything it's got to profit you. Every time if it's from the true God. It will always bless you. I can't say that enough. It will always bless you. It may bless somebody else, but it will always bless you. ALWAYS.

Otherwise, if you would start really abundantly sharing (giving) and you gave it to anybody else and you got nothing back the you would be the looser. God never works that way. The true God doesn't.

Though I give my body to be burned and do not have the love of God in the renewed mind in manifestation, it profits me nothing. And profit keeps you on the black side of the ledger. You know that when you prepare your taxes.

14

Boy, what a tremendous section of word.

Now watch verse four. The love of God in the renewed mind gets really Ticked off at other people? No? Then What? It can stand people. And I tell you, sometimes, I wish he'd left that out of the word. Sometimes the hardest thing in the world is to stand people, isn't it?

1 Corinthians 13:4
Charity suffereth long, *and* is kind; charity envieth not; charity vaunteth not itself, is not puffed up

The word of God in the renewed mind in manifestation suffers long. And, the love of God in the renewed mind in manifestation is kind. Sometimes I feel like I don't want to be kind. I'd like to hit them with a ball bat. Sock that old mule between the ears with a 2X4 of something. But I can't do it. If you really have the love of God in the renewed mind you just put up with people.

It envieth not, doesn't envy. The love of god in the renewed mind in manifestation envieth not. To envy is for me to want what rightfully belongs to you. "O gosh I wish I had it, I wish I had it and you didn't have it." That's envy!

The love of God in the renewed mind in manifestation vaunteth not itself. It's not on an ego trip. It's not a rash type of thing. The love of God in the renewed mind is not an egotist thing, oh; I want it, Rocky wants it.

And then this love of God in the renewed mind in manifestation is not puffed up. Look at me. Look how much of the knowledge of the word I have. I've studied the word for over 40 years and you've only studied it for 30 years. I've take a dozen classes and you've inly taken eleven. The love of

God in the renewed mind is not puffed up, doesn't have an ego trip going on.

Verse 5 says this love of God in the renewed mind in manifestation does not behave itself unseemly. That means take off all your clothes in public. It means wearing a $10,000 mink fur to a Sunday night fellowship. That's right! Because you'd be totally out of order.

1 Corinthians 13:5
doth not behave itself unseemly, seeketh not her own, is not easily provoked, thinketh no evil

It doesn't behave itself unseemly. It doesn't do things to draw attention to him, or her, self. It doesn't behave itself that way.

Seeketh not her own. Is not easily provoked. It doesn't say you don't get provoked, it just says it is not easily provoked. Because there comes a time in your walk with God that you better get provoked (it says so in the word too). But it is not easily provoked. In other words, you let people sort of get out of line sometimes. But it finally gets to the place where you have to take a stand. You say, why you old "whited sepulchre", "let you without sin, you cast the first stone". I think Jesus said some of those things. "And he looked round about on them with anger". He wasn't easily provoked, but when he was provoked he was very provoked. That's right. And he looked them right in the eye and said, you hypocrite. You lousy, measly bird. But the love of God in the renewed mind in manifestation is not *easily* provoked. Some people have such hot tempers their hot before they ever ought to get hot. They blow their lid all the time. So when

16

you blow your lid you blow out, and you don't want to do that.

I wish they'd left the rest of this verse out, it's really difficult. Thinketh no evil. Oh lordy!

"Hey, I saw Maggie with Herman last night. And they were driving east of town and you know there's a Holiday Inn out there." Thinketh no evil. Right there is where I think sometimes we ought to stop. How many of us have come to the place that we no longer even think any evil? And until you do I wouldn't be pointing any finger at anybody else; cause your pointing three back at yourself. The love of God in the renewed mind, when you've really got it, thinketh no evil.

Look, either the word of God is the truth or it's a lie. Either it's possible for us to so love that we don't think evil or we better chuck the whole thing. You know why you haven't experienced it is because you haven't believed it's God's word. Otherwise you can so renew your mind, and have the love of God in the renewed mind in manifestation, that you just do not think evil. And again, the reason it hasn't happened to you is because the word of God is not real to you. You don't believe that's really the word of God. You think, oh that's nice but nobody can do it. Wait a minute; if nobody can do it then why is it in the word. Then God's a liar. I want to tell you that's God's no liar. But you and I live in a community and a society that's so dammedable and corrupt that all you ever hear is all evil about everybody.

How much good does anybody really say about anybody, really? When you meet the natural senses man out there what does he know? It's always bad. So-n-so cheated here, so-n-so did this, so-n-so said that. How many time have people really said, "man, did you hear about Maggie, how wonderful she is?" "Or Herman, how terrifically he blessed Alice last night?" No! But you know; "Herman, he doesn't tell the truth all the time, he's not trustworthy." So you build doubt in people all the time.

Thinketh no Evil. When you arrive at that place where you think no evil there will be times where people will take advantage of you. But suppose they do; so what! Makes no difference. And the reason they take advantage of you is because you're not seeing them as doing that evil thing to you, or to others, and therefore you're just not thinking. And low and behold all at once you wake up and find out you've been hit in the head with a sledge hammer of something. So what! Still it's thinketh no evil. That's the walk of the love of God in the renewed mind in manifestation. That's the greatest love that there is. That's the love of God in Christ Jesus loving. That's loving the unlovable. That's allowing people to walk on your feet until the learn to walk on their own. That's allowing your life to be a broken bread, or a broken body, for others until they learn to break their own bread of life. It's allowing people to lean on you until they learn to lean on God and cast all their cares on him for he cares for them, and then walk on their own.

You and I need to be what Christ was, and is. For he's seated at the right hand of God and its Christ in us. And we have to allow people to take advantage of us until they learn to take advantage only of the promises of the word that are available to them. It's an unbelievable walk, that's why I believe it. It's just so far beyond the senses world that when you really walk this way everybody thinks your nuts. Cause, you know, you've been riding a bicycle with crooked handle bars so long that's the normal way to ride it. But when you

18

dare to believe God's word and walk on the greatness of God's word you become a peculiar people in more than one way. Because people are not use to seeing people who really love God. Who really love him, who have the mind of Christ, who can forgive and who love, who think no evil. Boy how many hundreds, and hundreds, and hundreds of times have we gone through this with people. Where a girl or a boy stays out until two o'clock in the morning and mommy says, "oh, I wonder what my girls doing?" What she's doing at two she could just as easily do at nine thirty. Little early in the evening, but it's nice. It's just a head trip. "Oh my, I wonder if they've been in an accident?" Why think evil? I refuse to see the evil in people. I prefer to see the love of God in the renewed mind in manifestation in people. I just refuse to see the rest. I want to think only the best. I want to not think inequity; I want to rejoice in the truth that I see.

1 Corinthians 13:6
rejoiceth not in iniquity, but rejoiceth in the truth

Verse seven says this love of God beareth all things that are according to the word. Believeth all things that are according to the word. And it hopeth for all things that are according to the word. Because these endure forever.

1 Corinthians 13:7
beareth all things, believeth all things, hopeth all things, endureth all things.

Because these endure how long? Forever. In other words, I can endure all things. Why, because of verse eight. The love of God in the renewed mind in manifestation never fails.

1 Corinthians 13:8
Charity never faileth: but whether *there be* prophecies, they
shall fail; whether *there be* tongues, they shall cease; whether
there be knowledge, it shall vanish away.

It *never* fails. It *never* fails. There's very few people
really believe that. That's what the word says. If you don't
believe that throw out John 3:16, throw out all the rest of
them. The love of God in the renewed mind in manifestation
never fails. The reason people get tripped up at that is
because, at first, when you start into something it looks like it
may fail. From the senses man's point of view, and from the
natural man's point of view, he would say it's a failure. But
the word of God says that the love of God in the renewed
mind never fails. And therefore you don't make the
judgement now, you wait and see it come to pass sometime in
the future.

But where you hear prophecies there going to fail. This
word fail is cease. The prophecies are going to cease.
Tongues, speaking in tongues, they're going to cease,
terminate. Knowledge of the mystery, it shall vanish away.

Verse nine.

1 Corinthians 13:9
For we know in part, and we prophesy in part.

Right now, we only know in part. We only prophesy in
part. But, in contrast, when that which is perfect is come,
which is the return of Christ, then that which is in part will
end. But until that time there will be speaking in tongues,
interpretation of tongues and prophecy.

1 Corinthians 13:10
But when that which is perfect is come, then that which is in part shall be done away.

You see, when you are a child you can play with a little motorcycle. When you get to be a man maybe they'll give you a Harley 74. The real McCoy.

1 Corinthians 13:11
When I was a child, I spake as a child, I understood as a child, I thought as a child: but when I became a man, I put away childish things.

When I was a child I played with a motorcycle like a child. But when I became a man I put away childish things and began to play with big boy toys. When I became a man I put away childish things, this is contingent on verse ten. When that which is perfect is come that which is in part shall be done away with.

Now we speak in tongues, interpret, prophesy. Operate word of knowledge, word of wisdom and discerning of spirits, faith, miracles and healings. All of the manifestations. But it's all in part. When that which is perfect is come then you will no longer need that because you'll have all the perfection of the presence of Christ in that new body. Then you don't need those toys, spiritually speaking.

1 Corinthians 13:12
For now we see through a glass, darkly; but then face to face: now I know in part; but then shall I know even as also I am known.

For now, with all the manifestations and all the greatness of the word, we see through a glass, and the word glass is mirror, darkly. The old mirrors are kind of shaded, smoky. That's what he's saying here. We see as in an old mirror, kind of smoky or hidden. But then. Then when? That which is perfect is come. Then we shall see face to face. Now I know in part, but then, again when that which is perfect is come, shall I know even as also I am known.

1 Corinthians 13:13
And now abideth faith, hope, charity, these three; but the greatest of these is charity.

And now, right now in our day and in our time, abideth *pistis*, believing. In the King James it is translated faith, the word is *pistis*, believing. Hope, the love of God in the renewed mind in manifestation. The greatest of these is the love of God in the renewed mind in manifestation. Isn't that something!

In a brief form I want to define these. Faith, or believing, is that which is available to you. Hope is that which you cannot receive now, it's future. But it's the love of God in the renewed mind which activates both your believing for that which is available now, and your hope of that which is still future.

Now abideth believing, hope and the love of God in the renewed mind. The greatest, the greatest, the greatest, the greatest of these in the body of the church, the born-again believers, is the love of God in the renewed mind in manifestation.

It's got to be. It thinketh no evil, is not puffed up, seeketh not her own, doesn't rejoice in inequity, beareth all things, believeth all things, hopeth all things.

Thinketh no evil. That's the love of God in the renewed mind in manifestation. So if you're going to try any new year's resolutions I'd try 1 Corinthians 13. You don't have to make your own, they're already written.

That's the greatness of the word of God. And we need to just remind ourselves that the word of God is the will of God. And inside the body of believers the greatest thing we can manifest is the love of God in the renewed mind. You can tell me how much you pray, or how often you go to church, or how much you share financially; but this is all nothing if you don't have the love of God in the renewed mind in manifestation.

I want to see your love. I want to see your tenderness, your forgiveness, your understanding. I want to see your heart. That's why we are to be kind one to another. The scriptures say be especially good to the household of faith. Sometimes it seems that people can be kind to everybody else, but not to their own brothers and sisters. The word of God says we are to be especially good to the household of faith. It says I have to love all those other people, it doesn't say I have to like them. But it says I have to be especially good to other believers in the household of faith. If I'm not going to be especially good to the believers who am I going to be especially good too? What a counterfeit I would be if I was especially good to some nincompoop out there that doesn't believe there's a God in heaven, much less cares and raises hell all the time. And for you who really want to love God, and serve God, I'm always nasty to you, it would profit me nothing.

Every time, when it's the greatness and truth of God's word, it will always profit you. Because God's no Indian-giver. It will always bless you, may bless somebody else too, but it will always you. And that's the joy of serving, that's the joy of living that life which is more than abundant with the love of God in the renewed mind in manifestation, THAT THINKETH NO EVIL.

PART TWO

Living Abundantly

SNT 0349
July 14, 1968

Before you were converted, born again of God's spirit, you were a man or woman of only body and soul. The man of body and soul has a mind, he has free will. Everything that ever comes to that human mind comes by way of one or another of the five senses; seeing, hearing, tasting, touching or smelling. Now when you were converted, born again, or saved; when you accepted the Lord Jesus Christ as your personal lord and saviour, believed God raised him from the dead, you received the spirit of Christ within, but your mind was not affected. The moment you were born again you still had the same mind you had one second before you were born again.

If something has never existed there is one word used in the bible with a mathematical exactness and a scientific precision; which God uses over, and over, and over again to describe the reality of bringing into concretion, bringing into existence that which has never been before, and that is the word "creation."

Your mind, however; has been in existence, and as man endeavors to change his life, to tap into resources that are more meaningful, more in concretion, more definite, there is a word used in the bible again with a very great exactness, and that is the word "renewed."

You cannot renew anything unless you first have it. You could not renew your mind if you had not had a mind to begin with.

Now there is one thing you cannot renew, and that is the spirit; because the spirit you never had to start with. When man is born he is body and soul. He does not have a spirit until he is born again. And no person is born again until they are obedient to the record that is given in Romans 10:9, that if you will confess with your mouth that Jesus is Lord and that God raised him from the dead.

This is a great reality, to confess with your mouth that Jesus is Lord, not to confess your sins. You can confess your sins until your blue in the face and still go home unsaved. Because you do not get saved by confessing your sin, because confessing your sin is work, hard word. And the word of God says we are saved by grace, not of works, lest any man should boast. So we do not confess our sin, we confess the saviour from sin, the Lord Jesus Christ.

When we confess with our mouths that Jesus is Lord, and believe in our hearts the God raised him from the dead, at that moment we are saved. And for God to save us he has to do one thing, bring in to concretion that which has never existed before which is spirit, and this he has to create.

Now once you're born again of God's spirit you are body, soul and spirit. You still have a mind, like you have a body. Now this mind, after you're born again of God's spirit, can be renewed. And it's in the renewing of the mind that you have the key to power. If you want to tap into the promises of God you've got to renew your mind. And this mind must be renewed according to the word of God and not according to what people say, or some theologians, or some preachers, or what anyone else may talk about. It's got to be according to God's rule book, his regulations.

There are two kinds of knowledge in this world. One kind of knowledge deals with information gathered via the five senses. And this knowledge is called natural knowledge. There's another kind of knowledge in this world which is gathered by way of the spirit. By the operation of the manifestations of the spirit. And this is called spiritual knowledge. It has become difficult for most men to live by the spirit side. Because we have become so acclimatized to living by our senses that we have just had a great difficulty to live by the spirit. And one of the reasons we've had a great difficulty to live by the spirit is because nobody taught us. It isn't that we wouldn't have done it, it isn't that we were not hungry, we just got turned off by all the bologna that everybody was handing out, and nobody was really teaching us how to tap in to God's power and promises.

When I teach I like to have a glass of water available. It is here and I know how to tap into it. But if I didn't know how to drink it, or that it was available, I couldn't satisfy a thirst if I had one.

One of the curses of our day and of our time is that nobody is teaching us, basically, how to tap into the riches of God's word, they just tell us what to do, but they don't teach us how.

You can tell a fella to pray till he's blue in the face; it doesn't do him anything but a discredit by telling him. Teach someone how to pray, then you're helping them. If they want to pray they can, and if they don't want to they don't have to.

It's like telling a man he ought to get saved. It doesn't do any good unless you tell him how to get saved. Then if he wants to he can and if he doesn't want to, well that's up to him.

You can tap into spiritual realities with the same exactness that you can tap into any sense knowledge fact in concretion in our world. Because you can develop your spiritual perception beyond anything you have ever dreamed of. It's there, it's latent, it's potential, but you're going to have to learn the principals, and then utilize the principals to bring the spiritual perception more efficaciously into concretion in your life day after day and week after week.

This is why it is difficult for men to learn the spiritual side because they have lived by their senses for so long. They know how to evaluate things in the senses realm but they do not know how to evaluate things in the spiritual realm or how to receive it. And so spiritually we just go through life empty. We talk about it but we know that we have not really tapped in.

When you were converted, born again, you had a new spirit created within you, but your mind was not affected. Everything that comes to your mind comes by way of one of the five senses. The spirit was created within you, but the mind has to be renewed.

The senses can send the information to the mind that can renew the mind. If you want to renew your mind you apply the same principals to the renewing of the mind that you would use in any other segment or category of learning. You renew the mind by changing what you're feeding on. By the information that you send up to your mind. If you do not like the crop you're reaping the only way you're going to change the crop you're reaping is by changing the seed you are sowing. Same thing in the spiritual world. If we're not satisfied with what we're tapping into we just got to change a little bit. And your will determines exactly what you're going to do in the category of the renewed mind.

How far you go with God will be dependent upon how far you determine you want to go, you will to go. Because under the true God nobody ever oversteps your will, and you, by the freedom of you will make up your own mind as to how far you want to go.

The renewed mind is the key to power in every individual believer's life. Look at Romans 12.

> Romans 12:1aa
> I beseech you therefore, brethren, by the mercies of God, that ye present your bodies a living sacrifice...

A living sacrifice, not a dead sacrifice, but a living sacrifice. I'm sick and tired of people who say, "well, I'd die for the Lord." What good is dying going to do. He didn't ask us to die for him, he ask us to be living sacrifices. You can't do anything for him if your dead. A living sacrifice is someone who has willingly made up his mind to sacrifice himself for others so that they too may live.

> Romans 12:1ff
> ... holy, acceptable unto God, *which is* your reasonable service.

Reasonable in the original texts is religious. It is our religious service to be a living sacrifice.

Romans 12:2aa
And be not conformed to this world...

Do you know how we get conformed to the world; the same way we get conformed to the greater things, by what somebody else teaches us. No man can go beyond where he is led. The reason I'm at the place in my life is because of where I've been led, what I've been taught. No man can ever rise above what he is taught. No man can ever believe any bigger that what he is taught. And no man can ever lead you except where he himself has ever gone. Remember Jesus' statement about the blind leading the blind that they both end up in the ditch. Well some of us have been there a couple of times in life, haven't we? We thought we were living and walking with people that had 20/20 vision but they didn't. We ended up in the ditch, but God, in his great wisdom and grace made a way to get us out.

Romans 12:2ff
... but be ye transformed by the renewing of your mind, that ye may prove what *is* that good, and acceptable, and perfect, will of God.

Transformed here in Romans 12 is the same word as transfigured in the gospels when Jesus was transfigured before Peter and James and John on the mount of transfiguration. Be transformed by one thing, get a new figure in your mind, by renewing your mind. Why? That you might be able to prove what is that good and acceptable and perfect will of God. The perfect will of God can never be proven in any other way than by a man, who must be born again of God's spirit, and renewing his mind according to the greatness of the revelation and living it in concretion day by day.

Romans 13:14

But put ye on the Lord Jesus Christ, and make not provision for the flesh, to *fulfil* the lusts *thereof.*

Whatever we can put on cannot be in the category of the spirit, it has to be in the category of the mind. We are to put on the Lord Jesus Christ. Where can I put him on? I can't put him on in the spirit, logically there is only one place I can put him on, and that is above my ears, in my mind.

Ephesians 4:22aa

that ye put off concerning the former conversation the old man...

Whatever we put on we can take off. Here God is telling us to put off the old man. Where is the old man? He is in the mind. It is called the old man because it is the mind you have been developing since the day you were born. It is everything you have learned via your five senses. But now, after that you were born again, you have the ability to put on the mind of Christ. That's why the mind is referred to as the old man in the bible. But now you have a new man, Christ in you. And that mind of Christ, that you can have after you are born again, is called the new man.

Ephesians 4:23

and be renewed in the spirit of your mind

The word spirit here in verse 23 is the word life. Be renewed in the life of your mind.

Ephesians 4:24

and that ye put on the new man, which after God is created in righteousness and true holiness.

Put on the new man which after God is created. Remember we were originally only body and soul. When we were born again, when we confessed with our mouth the Lord Jesus and believed in our hearts that God raised him from the dead, God created in us spirit. That spirit is created in righteousness and true holiness. That's what gives us the ability to put on the new man in our minds. The new birth puts us in harmony and alignment, in a perpendicular relationship, with God.

Philippians 2:5
Let this mind be in you, which was also in Christ Jesus

When we have the mind of Christ in our mind, we have the renewed mind. Look at how Jesus lived; "I and my father are one," "I always do my fathers will."

Colossians 3:1
If ye then be risen with Christ, seek those things which are above, where Christ sitteth on the right hand of God

It is my sincere prayer that you put off that old man mind and put on the new man mind, that you can become a better workman for God.

PART THREE

Christic Formed in You

SNT 732, November 24, 1974

I've been thinking about how Christ is formed within us, and that's what I want to open up with, and share with you. Every earthly father who is a real Christian and loves his children desires, within the inner most part of his being, to reproduce himself in his children. The heart of Christianity is the Father God, through Jesus Christ, building Himself in us through His revealed Word, so that our moment-by-moment living is like and is with the Master. In Ephesians 5 it says:

> Ephesians 5:1-2
> 1 Be ye therefore followers of God, as dear children;
>
> 2 And walk in love, as Christ also hath loved us, and hath given himself for us an offering and a sacrifice to God for a sweetsmelling savor.

God so loved, according to John – remember? – 3:16? God so loved that He gave. All love is giving. God, the Creator of all heaven and earth, so loved that He gave His only begotten Son, that whosoever believeth in him should not perish, but have everlasting life.

The reason it's everlasting life is because it has a starting point for you. The reason it's eternal life is because it has no starting point for God. And therefore, that which you receive from God is eternal, but for you it's everlasting. That is the difference in the usage of the two words "everlasting" and "eternal." With God, that which you receive is eternal. But for you, it's everlasting because it had a starting point. If you were twenty-five before you were born again, then before that time you had no everlasting life. But when you were born again of God's spirit at twenty-five, from then on you have His eternal life. But it's everlasting from that point on for you.

We walk in love "as Christ also hath loved us." He who knew no sin became sin, so that you and I might become the righteousness of God in him. Imagine that. God so loved that He gave. Jesus Christ so loved that he gave. And you and I must so love that we have to give. I have to love to the point where people learn to love because of the love that I share with them. That's what I mean when I say, you have to learn to let people walk on your feet until they learn to walk on their own.

You have to be the hands of people until they learn to use their own hands. You have to be the heart of people until people learn to use their heart and extend it out to the lives of other people. We have to be broken bread for people until they learn to break their own Bread of Life.

God so loved, Christ loved and we have to so love because, "he hath given himself for us an offering, a sacrifice to God for a sweetsmelling savor..." – and that is better than Chanel No. 5. And the Word says that we are to God a sweet smell. When this Christ is formed within us to the end that we love with the love wherewith he loved – and it is possible to love the unlovable, it is possible to so renew your mind, that there is absolutely nothing that any other Christian believer does but that you still love them and don't criticize and find fault with them.

You see, we've got to go to the Word and love with the love wherewith Christ Jesus loved. And you're never going to get to that place unless you commit yourself to the integrity of God and His Word and let this Word be built in you. And the building of the Word takes time. It's not something you take a class on in two weeks, and walk away and say, "Well now I've got it. The rest of my life I can fool around." That's just the bare foundation. It gives you all the principles on which to build, that I know. But the building takes time. Like building this Biblical Research Center takes time. If we were going to manufacture a piano – you could have all the things to put in a piano – it still takes time to put it together. And in that process of learning and growing, where people move from hearing the Word to building the Word within their lives, takes time. And that takes a lot of love.

Think of the love God had in Christ Jesus to make salvation available to us. To make it possible for us to be born again of God's spirit, to be filled with the holy spirit, to have a knowledge of His Word so we could rightly divide it and operate manifestations decently and in order so that all of God's people could be edified, built up, by way of exhortation and comfort. To hear from God Almighty, the Creator of heaven and earth.

In Acts Chapter 16 there's a record of two men of God. And the same God that was in those two men is the same God that's in you. The same Jesus Christ – the same yesterday, today and forever.

Acts 16:16-17
16 And it came to pass, as we went to prayer, a certain damsel [young lady] possessed with a spirit of divination met us, [who] brought her masters much

gain by soothsaying [palm reading kind of stuff, you know; other things]:

17 The same followed Paul and us, and cried, saying, these men are the servants of the most high God, [who] show unto us the way of salvation.

Was she right in what she said? Absolutely. Don't tell me that devil spirits don't know. What she was saying was right on. Most people would give her a front row seat.

Acts 16:18-25
18 And this did she many days. But Paul, being grieved, turned and said to [the woman? No. He said to what?] the spirit [the spirit, that devil spirit, he said] I command thee in the name of Jesus Christ to come out of her. And he [the devil spirit] came out [of her] the same hour [That means pronto, right away, quick].

19 And when her masters saw that the hope of their gains was gone, they caught Paul and Silas, and drew *them* into the marketplace [or to the court] unto the rulers,

20 And brought them to the magistrates, saying, These men, being Jews, do exceedingly trouble our city,

21 And teach customs, which are not lawful for us to receive, neither to observe, being Romans.

22 And the multitude rose up together against them [against Paul and Silas]: and the magistrates rent off their clothes [you know, they're getting real hot under the collar] and commanded to beat *them*.

23 And when they had laid many stripes upon them, they cast *them* into prison, charging the jailor to keep them safely:

24 Who, having received such a charge, thrust them into the inner prison [so they *couldn't* get out], and made their feet fast in the stocks.

25 And at midnight Paul and Silas prayed, and sang praises unto God: and the prisoners heard them

"And at midnight Paul and Silas" ...moped. They said, "Oh God, we're working for you, why do we have to suffer like this? Lord, all we were doing is your will. You gave us revelation, it was a devil spirit, we took it out." No, at midnight Paul and Silas, prayed. Under the most adverse conditions, being in prison for something they shouldn't have been in prison for at all, yet at midnight:

Acts 16:25-30
25 And at midnight Paul and Silas prayed, and sang praises unto God: and the prisoners heard them

26 And suddenly there was a great earthquake, so that the foundations of the prison were shaken: and immediately all the doors were opened, and every one's bands were loosed.

27 And the keeper of the prison awaking out of his sleep, and seeing the prison doors open, he drew out his sword, and would have killed himself, supposing that the prisoners had [all, what?] been fled.

28 But Paul cried with a loud voice, saying, Do thyself no harm: for we are all here.

29 Then [the jailer] called for a light [he got his little lantern, his six-cell], and sprang in, and came trembling, and fell down before Paul and Silas,

30 And brought them out, and said, Sirs, what must I do to be saved?

What a record. God so loved, Jesus Christ so loved, Paul and Silas so loved that even though they had laid many stripes upon them, cast them into prison: they sang hymns, they praised the Lord, they prayed. And when this thing occurred, the jailer said, "Fellas, I want that stuff you've got. I want to tap into the same thing you've got. What must I do to be saved?

Acts 16:31-33
31 And they said, Believe on the Lord Jesus Christ, and thou shalt be saved, and thy house.

32 And they spake unto him the word of the Lord [that's the only thing that saves people], and to all that were [what?] in his house.

33 And he [the jailer] took them the same hour of the night, and washed *their* stripes; and was baptized he and all [of] his [household], straightway.

That means immediately. They were born again of God's spirit – that whole household – that night.

Acts 16:34
And [then] when he had brought them into his house, he rejoiced, believing in God with all his house.

Paul and Silas did not cry because the magistrates threw them in prison. They didn't go around complaining. They knew they had to be broken bread until the people learned to break their own. They knew they had to be able to take it until people could take on Christ for themselves.

You and I have to so love, so have Christ formed within us, that we are the demonstration of the love of Christ in the renewed mind in manifestation.

In the book of Galatians, chapter 4, look at verse 19.

Galatians 4:19
My little children, of whom I travail in birth again until Christ be formed in you,

This was the walk of the Apostle Paul. They were born again of God's spirit. They were already "children," but they were little kids spiritually. You can be 90 years old and just be a little child spiritually, just sort of like a pledge or a fledgling. And the Word says, "My little children of whom I travail in birth." It's like in Genesis where it says something about "in sorrow thou shalt bring forth children." That's a bunch of baloney. The Word says "in labor." But being Occidental, and everybody having to suffer like crazy having kids, so we've got to get the word "sorrow" in there. No, it is "labor." That it isn't "sorrow" in Genesis, it is "labor," which is true. Any woman who has a baby is going to put in at least 15 minutes of labor to get the production, I suppose. But look at what he's saying, "children of whom I travail in birth [in labor, in birth] again." "Again." They're already born again of Christ's spirit. Christ is in them. But Christ is not formed in their mind. The new birth is "Christ in you, the hope of glory." But putting it on is to get the form of Christ in your mind. So that when you speak you speak like Christ would speak, that when you smile you would smile like Christ would smile, you'd love like Christ would love, you'd share his peace like Christ would share his peace.

Philippians 2:13
For it is God [It is who? God.] which worketh in you [it is God who is at work within you] to will and to do of his good pleasure.

God at work within us. Spiritually he is at work within us that we may will and do His good pleasure. Now to know what is God's pleasure you must know God's Word. And one of the things that is God's pleasure, is certainly to love with the love wherewith He loved, the tenderness wherewith He was tender, the joy with which He joyed, the blessings with which He blessed, the thanksgiving with which He lived. It is God at work within us to will and to do His good pleasure.

You see, God is building His love life in you. His righteousness, His strength, His perfection, His goodness, His justice, His forgiveness. God is at work within you to build that within you so that you can share it with others.

In II Peter is a tremendous truth.

II Peter 3:18
But grow in grace, and in the knowledge of our Lord and Saviour Jesus Christ...

Grow in grace. The word "grace" literally could be translated, "love's gifts." Grace is always God, who is love, at work. Love at work is grace. It says "grow in grace, and in the knowledge of our Lord and Saviour, Jesus Christ." It doesn't say, "grow in the knowledge of Scripture." The Christian world is loaded with that stuff, at times, but no love. We've got grads of bible seminaries I wish had never be taught. All they do is prance around showing people how much knowledge of the Scriptures they have, and make everybody else that hasn't got that knowledge feel bad.

My goodness. Why did we ever teach them God's Word? Breaks my heart. It's not the knowledge of the Scripture you know, but the extent to which you know him and walk in the love wherewith he loved. Nothing wrong with knowledge of the Scripture. But it looks to me you haven't got enough knowledge if you don't apply it. And you ought to read a few verses that tell you how to put it on – how to love with the love wherewith he loved, how to forgive with the forgiveness wherewith he forgives, how to keep your tongue under control so you don't go blabbing everything all the time.

It's an unruly evil, remember? The tongue. No man can tame it. So quit trying to tame it, let God tame it. He's the only one that can do it. Otherwise you're always going to have the running off of the tongue, and diarrhea of the mouth. So... Grow in grace. That growing in grace is to grow in the love life of Christ. Like you can grow in the new birth. You can't get more spiritually. The growing of it is in the renewed mind and in the walk. Grow in grace – love at work in your life – by God through Christ, Who saved us when we were totally dead in trespasses and sins without God and without hope. He loved us enough that He saved us.

Can you and I really, if we know what that means, do less than endeavor to build the grace of God in our minds, and the love wherewith He loved, to share that love? So it's not a knowledge of the Scriptures, but what do I love? How do I love with that knowledge?

I Corinthians 2:9-10

9 but as it is written, Eye hath not seen, nor ear heard, neither have entered into the heart of man, the things which God hath prepared for them that love him.

10 But [Yet] God hath revealed [the things] unto us by his Spirit; for the Spirit searcheth all things, yea, the deep things of God.

"God hath prepared for them that," Love Him. He has revealed to them by His spirit. And it's the spirit that searches the deep things of God. And with God at work in you to will and to do of His good pleasure, when you and I renew our minds and walk in the light of that Word, then we are having Christ formed in us.

People will never see Christ, until they see you – he's seated in the heavenlies, waiting to get back. The only Christ they'll ever see is the walk within you – the Christ in you. The joy in you, the thanksgiving, the blessing, the effervescence, the enthusiasm, the smile, the dedication, the commitment. That's all they'll ever see of Christ. They're not going to open the Book (bible). They'll buy one, put it in the house – they ain't gonna open it. Not going to read it. Not going to study it. But they're going to look at your life, and they're going to look at mine. And they are going to say, "Does he really love? He talks about forgiveness; does he really forgive? You see, they'll never see Christ until they see it in you, see it in me. We have to become Christ-filled, Christ-centered. Christ everything, must be within us. Whether we're in a shop, or a factory, or in a car, or sitting on a log, it has to be Christ in manifestation.

> Ephesians 3:8
> Unto me, who am less than the least of all saints, is this grace given, that I should preach among the Gentiles the unsearchable [untrackable] riches of Christ;

There are some things in life that you can track. Maybe one of these mornings we'll have some snow, and if the rabbits have been out that night, I guarantee you, you can track them. But there are other things that, in the Word of God, that cannot be tracked.

Some things you can track. Having been in research all these years, there are some things I can put together, as I've heard it said, "with a mathematical exactness and a scientific precision" – that when I'm finished with it I'm absolutely positive, if God's Word is right, that there's nobody can touch it. Because I can just track it, like a rabbit, to where he is sitting underneath the bush or the woodpile. Track him right in. But then there are other things in God's Word that are absolutely untrackable. That's this word "unsearchable." That word "unsearchable" is the word "untrackable." The grace given, "that I should preach among the Gentiles the unsearchable, or the untrackable, riches of Christ." I don't understand it, but I sure appreciate it. I can't explain it, but I sure love Him for it. But there are a lot of other things much simpler than the riches of Christ that I can't explain either. Electricity is one. I've had a real problem trying to explain it. But I sure enjoy it when I need it for the darkness to be dispelled, when I need toast in the morning, and a few other things.

You see, that love of God tenderizes you. That love of God, when Christ is formed within you, makes you forgiving, makes you tender, makes you kind, makes you understanding – because it couldn't do anything else but.

Colossians 1:9-10
9 For this cause we also, since the day we heard *it*, do not cease to pray for you, and to desire that ye might be filled with the knowledge of his will in all wisdom and spiritual understanding.

10 That ye might walk worthy of the Lord unto all pleasing, being fruitful [and to be fruitful is to propagate oneself, literally in the text] in every good work, and [growing up, "increasing" is "growing up by"] the knowledge of God [by the knowledge of God].

Walk worthy of the Lord unto all, pleasing. You see, there's a walk with the Lord and there's a walk in the world. It's a two-fold walk. It's a walk with him, but there's also a walk in the world. And we're to so walk worthy of the Lord in the world unto all pleasing, propagating ourselves and growing up. Growing up. I know that this Christ in you the hope of glory is perfect. I know it's eternal life from God's point of view. I know all that. But I know people, born again of God's spirit, who have an absolute miserable existence. Who are full of fear and worry and anxiety and frustration, downcast and defeated. People, that cannot be right-on. For our Christ came and lived within us that we might have a life which is more than abundant. That we might be more than conquerors. "I can do all things through Christ who infuses inner strength into me" (as one translator puts it) "who strengthens me." What a tremendous record from God's Word.

Philippians 4:11
Not that I speak in respect of want: for I have learned, in whatsoever state [King James says] I am, therewith ... content.

That's not true. That would say if you're sick, be thankful you're sick. And if you're dying, be thankful you're dying. That's a bunch of baloney. The text reads, "in whatsoever state, I am self-adequate." That makes you more than a conqueror. More than an abundant life. In whatever "state." Your standing is one of a son of God. State fluctuates. In whatever state I am self-adequate. Not because of my own self, but because of His self: God at work within me to will and to do what? His good pleasure. He makes me self-adequate, don't you see it? That's why I am adequate. Because of His adequacy, His ability, His willingness, His desire.

I too had to learn to love, like everybody else. It said "growing up," right? I too had to grow up. Because there was a long time I took growing up. Especially with some people, I had an awful time growing up with them – that I had to love them. It was so much easier to get mad at them all the time, and raise hell with them. Because I just didn't like the way they combed their hair or put on their pants or what kind of shoes they wore. And golly-sixty, to find someone unlovable and then the Word says you have to love them. That is a real strain on your head. I too had to learn. I've always had, in the inner part of my being, I guess, the ability to understand a lot of things about people. But that love wherewith I love today is just unbelievable even for me. I'm like that vessel we read about, I know this. It can only be God at work within me that brought me to that place. Because there's nothing anybody could tell me that would shock me, number one. Nobody. You couldn't tell me anything you've done that could even shock me. And you couldn't tell me anything you've done that'd make me think less of you to the end that I wouldn't love you. And for God to do that within me takes an awful big God.

I've come to the place where, I trust, by God's mercy and grace I am today, that there is just nobody that I could not love. Has to be God. And I can so easily put up with the shortcomings of people – I'm talking now about Christians who are also growing up – because God tenderized me on the inside because of the greatness of His love. If He can take a man that is calloused and hard and egotistical – and all the rest of the junk that goes with the usual academic procedures – and so bring him to the place...that is how I got to it. Just by growing up in the Word and by letting this Word live in my mind and by practicing the presence of God – by the Word all the way through. This is why Galatians speaks so loudly to my heart.

> Galatians 2:20
> I am ["I was," is the text] crucified with Christ; nevertheless I live; yet not I, but Christ liveth in me: and the life which I now live in the flesh [the senses world] I live by the faith [*pistis*] of the Son of God, who loved me, and gave himself for me.

I was crucified with Christ. When Christ was crucified I was crucified with him and so were you. When he died we died with him. And the Word says when he was laid into the sepulcher we were laid there with him; when he arose we arose with him; when he ascended we ascended with him. That is why the Word says we are already seated in the heavenlies in Christ Jesus. Because wherever Christ was, we were. Where he is, we are. When he comes back, where he will be we will be, for he is our Savior and our Lord. I was crucified with Christ, nevertheless I am alive. Yet not I, but Christ lives in me. That is the greatness of this life. And the life which I now live, right now in the senses world, I live by the *pistis*, the believing, of Jesus Christ, who so loved me that he gave himself for me.

As far as I understand a little bit from the Word about building the greatness of this Word in your life: what I have seen, through the years, is that the only men and women who grow deeply spiritual are men and women who allow the Word to be fully declared unto them and who walk in the fullness of the greatness of that Word. These are the men and the women who become deeply spiritual. I did not say "religious." I said "spiritual." And it is that Word living in you and you living in the Word – manifesting forth the greatness of it – that moves the greatness of the power of God in our world today.

This is Christmas week. That is why I wanted to share this message about Christ being formed in you. Because this is what our nation needs. This is what your next-door neighbor needs: to see that Christ in you with the love of God in the renewed mind in manifestation. There is nothing so completely satisfying as the knowledge of the Word in the renewed mind in manifestation, bringing that love to people. You will never be so blessed in your life until you are blessed by helping somebody else with the love that Christ has given you. You will never be so blessed until you learn to forgive like Christ has forgiven you. To bring peace to someone's soul because Christ first brought it to you.

That is why my prayer too is that Christ be formed in you. That we can so love that we will be wonderful men and women of God who the world can look at, and if they want to see, they can.

PART FOUR

Love in the Household

SNT 0683, May 5, 1974

Take your bibles tonight, please, and go to Philippians, chapter one. This great record in God's Word that I want to share as a foundational scripture that I'd like to build something with you tonight. It's so singularly significant because it's so apropos to our day and to our time. Verse 27 of chapter one.

> Philippians 1:27
> Only let your conversation be as it becometh the gospel of Christ: that whether I come and see you, or else be absent, I may hear of your affairs, that ye stand fast in one spirit, with one mind striving together for the faith of the gospel;

This was the record that God directed Paul to send to the Philippians because they had committed some practical error and he was just straightening it out for them. And the walk that is the walk of unity, the walk of one mind, has to be a walk that's just done day after day and moment after moment and week after week. I wanted to show our people again that if the greatness of God's Word is to live in our day and in our time, we have to stand together in the household, with one mind, in the unity of Christ Jesus. You can't be flitting around from one little ole group here, there, and yonder, and expect the greatness of God's Word to move in our lifetime.

Paul knew this, what had occurred among the Philippians at the time, they said "well, it's a wonderful gospel, we'll do it over here, we'll do it over there, and one little group over there trip, and this little group over here have got the same gospel we're doing. Paul said to them by divine revelation, he said that, whether I come and see you or else be absent, I may hear of your affairs that you stand fast in one spirit, with one mind, striving together for **THE** faith; which is the faith of Jesus Christ, the gospel of faith. That's that good news of that wonderful faith of our Lord and Saviour Jesus Christ. This unity is that one body. It's the household of God, it's the family of faith that the Word of God speaks about.

I use a phrase many times all over the country, I guess, among our people, you've heard me use it. I'm sure you have if you've been around any length of time. Where I simply will come up, at times, and I may say, "well God bless you. I love you. You're the best." And then I keep right on walking. A few of you I'm sure have heard it. Many times, people think this is just a flipping thing with me. but it isn't. To me it is exactly what I mean, and I mean what I say. God bless. I love you. And you're the best. that's the unity, that's that one body. That's that one mind that you and I must have if we're going to move the integrity and the greatness of God's word among God's people. All of us here at International that are on the staff, research, and working in research, this kind of thing, when it comes to the Word of God. I think all of us are absolutely convinced, without a shadow of a doubt, that the greatness of God's Word, as it was given in the first century, had pretty well washed itself out by 110 AD. And there has been no greatness of God's Word available to the people in any great amount since that day. Then you have a right to say, then how come the Christian church then is so voluminous, or has been so tremendous through the years? That's an honest question, I think it deserves an honest answer.

The honest answer is, as far as I understand history and the greatness of the Word, is that the only reason Christianity, so called, has taken over sections of the world, and promogulated itself, and moved across sections of the world, is because the nations that adopted it had the power structure, they had the money, and they had the influence to make it live, as they called it. Because in the early days, now early I'm back at 325 AD, that's not so early. But at 325 AD if you didn't become a Christian you got your head chopped off. Many died! And this one of the reasons why the so-called "Christians" have always carried the physical sword. Because the nations had the power, they had the money, they had the influence, and therefore they went everywhere, not with the greatness of the love of God in the renewed mind, one mind, one spirit. But look, we're Christians. We got the power, we got the money. Look how God's blessed us. therefore, you'd better be Christian, if you don't you get it (your head chopped off). So, it's got to be a phony. And in order to show its bigness it built buildings. Cathedrals. I understand now it's worked on one for 1,200 years, or 1,000 years, and it still isn't finished. The bible says God doesn't dwell in buildings made with hands.

You see, there's never been a great teaching of the Word! We have been impressed with big buildings, or other material things. Or that I've got the money, I've got the power, kind of trip. Rather than letting the greatness of God's Word live in manifestation. In the 10:30 session this morning I showed our people, again, from God's Word, that in the early church whenever somebody was born again they immediately spoke in tongues. Immediately! Today there's some people that if they hear about speaking in tongues they think you're going straight to hell. That's right. Yet, in the early church whenever somebody was born again they spoke in tongues. And this occurred all through that early days of the church until about 90 AD, and then it started waning. Because they got away from God's Word. When those men died, when Paul died. When John, the man who wrote the book of Revelation, passed away. The apostles were gone and the little groups, the splinter groups, grew here, there and yonder. And then they lost the integrity of the Word and it got to be in an area, the church of Rome, the church of Babylon, the church in Antioch, the church here, there and yonder.

So, when God directed the Apostles to send this word to the church of the Philippians, He had to do to them what He did to the church in Corinth. Give them a little reproof and correction, which is instruction in righteousness. Because all of God's Word is God breathed, and all of it is profitable for doctrine, which is right believing. Or reproof, reproving us where we are believing wrongly. And correcting us so we can get back on the ball for God.

In 2 Corinthians chapter 2, verse 4.

4 For out of much affliction and anguish of heart I wrote unto you with many tears; not that ye should be grieved, but that ye might know the love which I have more abundantly unto you.

This was a reproof and correction for the church in Corinth. Because they were not walking in that one mind, and in the unity of the one spirit. And he said he, "wrote to them with many tears." That means it hurt him to have to write it. And he wrote it not that they should greave about it, but that they might know, not question, but that the might know the love which he had more abundantly unto them, else he wouldn't have written them.

You see, the one body, that household of God, the family of faith. the greatest thing that has to be there to keep that unity going is the love of God in the renewed mind in manifestation. In John 3:16, and I don't think you have to look this one up, is that God so loved, who loved, God loved. GOD, that's the emphasis. For GOD so loved. The secondary emphasis is that He gave. God so loved that He gave. All true love always has giving in it.

You know it 1 John chapter 3 verse 1.

Behold, what manner of love the Father hath bestowed upon us, that we should be called the sons of God: therefore the world knoweth us not, because it knew him not.

God so loved that he gave. I'm a Christian born again of God's spirit, not by good works, but by grace. I am His because, he is worthy, and not because I was worthy. Because He saved me when I was dead in trespasses and sins, without God and without hope. Ladies and gentlemen, that's love. And if God so loved that he gave His only begotten son; and I behold what manor of love the father hath bestowed on us. To bestow is to lay it on a fella. It isn't that he earned it and then you hand it to him, it's unmerited grace and favor. Can I do less for the body of believers than to love? If God loved that He bestowed such love upon me that we should be called sons of God. Isn't that beautiful? What a great love.

Therefore, the world knoweth us not. I wonder how long we're going to have to live to figure that one out. It is so simple that most people go a lifetime and never get around to the great reality of the truth of it. They're still looking someway, or somehow or another to get the world to say yes, isn't that wonderful. It just plainly says, "the world knoweth us not." So do you think the world's ever going to back you up? If you do God's got to re-write His Word. And I'll bet you He's not going to do it. Because God knows, and you know it too, that there are only two powers in this whole world. They're both spiritual. One is the God and father of our Lord Jesus Christ, and the other god is the advisory, the devil. And everything is either of the one God or the other. There can't be both. The world knoweth us not. The world's not going to back this ministry. The world's not going to stand with us.

Seems like people get so impressed with names (you know). If the right reverend said so, or doctor so and so said so, or some politician said so, or some banker said so. Unless those people say what the Word says, they're in the opposite corner. God does not need the world to back up his word. The Word stands by itself. The world never backs that Word. They will use your life a little bit, if they can, to bring themselves more worldliness. It's a real temptation in the life of a man that the adversary keeps throwing at you. Where you can, for instance, go and meet with a certain group of senators, or representatives, and satan tells you, "man if you've got those fellows really walking the Word would live." I've got to read that in the book (Bible), haven't read it. But you see, it's a real temptation. So, unless you're walking in alignment and harmony you'll get caught in that stuff. I wouldn't mind teaching the Word to a few senators. But NOT because their senators but because they need God's Word! That's the reason for it.

You don't put your confidence in the world and in what is called worldly leaders. My bible says you pray for them, you don't put your confidence in them. I think it says that, doesn't it? Bless God, why don't we just believe the Word. There is not governor that is going to make this Word of God live; unless that Word of God lives in the governor. That's true! But I mean as, just from a professional point of view. No governor, no doctor, no lawyers, no banker, no preacher. Nobody except the Word lives in them. THE WORD! And when they walk on that Word then that unity is there, and they stay put in that household.

> 1 John 3:2
> Beloved, now are we the sons of God, and it doth not yet appear what we shall be: but we know that, when he shall appear, we shall be like him; for we shall see him as he is

Right now, we are the sons of God. Praise God. For that king of love, we ought to stand in the unity of that one mind. That one purpose, to move God's Word in our day and time.

Look at chapter 4, bless your hearts. Verse 15.

> 1 John 4:15
> Whosoever shall confess that Jesus is the Son of God, God dwelleth in him, and he in God.

The son of God! Is that what it says? How long do you waiver between two opinions? If you ever want to stand in the unity and with that one mind, this is a biggie! *"Whosoever shall confess that Jesus is the Son of God."* The SON of God. Is that what it says? Then that's what it means. God's Word stands, not man's opinion. The one that says that (that Jesus is the son God), what's it (the Word) say about that man? God dwelleth in him. And that man that says that, he is in God. That's right. Now you've got both of them. God in the man and the man in God. Anybody that says the opposite is off the ball somewhere. Either that, or God's Word is wrong. So why don't people quit arguing with God? Why don't they just believe God's Word? What a bunch of bologna.

Look at verse 16.

1 John 4:16-17
¹⁶ And we have known and believed the love that God hath to us. God is love; and he that dwelleth in love dwelleth in God, and God in him.

¹⁷ Herein is our love made perfect, that we may have boldness in the day of judgment: because as he is, so are we in this world.

"As He is so are we." Now He either lied or He told the truth people. The world will say to you, "Oh, that can't be." The old adversary will say to you, "you're not that good, you just can't be that successful." They'll say to you, "that's an ego trip, you need a psychiatrist." I don't think so. I think they need a psychiatrist! Outside of the Word, people, there's just no answer. *"As He is so are we in this world."* That's that one body, that unity. That family. The household, the family of faith.

1 John 4:18-19

[18] There is no fear in love; but perfect love casteth out fear: because fear hath torment. He that feareth is not made perfect in love.

[19] We love him, because he first loved us.

And this love is not that mother kind, or you know, floppy kind. No. It's the genuine love of God that's been shed abroad in your hearts by the holy spirit. You renew your mind on. And you just walk with that love. That love has reproof in it. Correction; which is instruction in righteousness. Like Paul did to the Philippians and over in Corinth.

Every tree that's a fruit bearing tree has its value because of the fruit it bears. Not just how pretty or decorative it can be, but by the fruit it produces. And God expects His people, in the unity of that one mind, to produce fruit. And you can't produce good fruit if the good qualities are lacking. You see, one of the fruits of the spirit, in Galatians 5:22 is love. The manifestations of the spirit produce the fruit. So until we see the manifestations, you can't have the good quality of the fruit.

When Reverend and Mrs. Townsend came in from New York a week ago today. Mrs. Townsend had brought with her a copy of the tape of her teaching at the women's advance in New York. She gave it to me and asked me if I would take the time to analyze it. And to criticize it, as she said, which means constructive recommendations on how to do it better. And I said, well I'll think about it. And I did. But, I did have an opportunity to listen to it. And I was just tremendously blessed with what I heard. Because, it's this kind of teaching that she was doing, and if the rest of our women across the country in their women's advances, are teaching the Word as great as that, which I'm sure their doing, I want to tell you, God must be building some of the greatest women the world has ever seen since the first century. And Mrs. Townsend was talking about how the Christians just don't come to God's Word. How that, they're always flipping out on it one way or the other. She used much better terminology than flipping out though, still Naomi. How, the world is a lie, the Word of God is truth. She said, everything the world says you just do the opposite of and you basically on God's Word. She said, how did we learn to have all these fears? The reason we learned it is because somebody taught us to be afraid.

I guess there are only two physically natural fears, one is the fear of falling and the other is loud noises. Well most of us have had a few more than that. Well how did we get them? We were taught. I was taught silly little things like if a black cat walks in front of you that means bad luck. If you walk underneath a ladder that's bad luck. If you sit on cement, you have hemorrhoids. Those are a few that I was taught. We learn to fear. Yet the bible says that perfect love casts out fear. You see, the world has absolutely no control over us. The reason it controls us is we've allowed it to control us. Because what the world says is absolutely contrary to what God says.

Why are people full of fear? Look, we read a little while ago, as He is so are we in this world. Why then are people full of fear? Somebody must have taught them the wrong stuff. Right? Why are you so worried? Somebody must have taught us wrongly. Why, you know, so many anxieties? Somebody must have taught us this. Why so much bitterness among the born-again believers? Why so much gossiping among the believers? Why so much criticism? You see, these are all poison to the human mind. And we are to be of one mind. And the one mind is the mind of the Word. The mind of Christ the word says. Transformed by the renewing of your mind (Rom. 12:2). How can people be so unforgiving? When God so loved the He gave, and he cleansed us. Where is it, in Ephesians, where He says He rescued us out from among. Just when we were ready to fall over the precipice, be killed, he rescued us. Snatched us. People are so full of guilt, born-again of God's spirit, and yet so full of guilt. Born of God's spirit and yet live under condemnation, when the Word of God says there is therefore **NO** condemnation to them that are in Christ Jesus. Who walk not after the flesh but after the spirit. NO CONDEMNATION! So then why do we live with that guilt? Why do we live with the condemnation? Because somebody taught it to us. And ladies and gentleman, that's opposite of the Word. Not what the Word says!

You know, the two great commandments; Jesus Christ reduced the whole mess to two you know. He stated them in Matthew 22:37 and following. Thou shalt what? Love the Lord thy God. Love God! Love God with all your heart, mind, soul and strength. And what? Your neighbor as yourself. Now how in the world can you love your neighbor if you don't love yourself? It says you love your neighbor as yourself. It's got to start with you honey. It's got to start with you sir. It's got to start with me. If I don't love myself how can I love my neighbor? And most people don't love themselves. They think their stinky, or something. And I don't mean Chanel #5. That's right! Because all their lifetime, all their lifetime, their living like in the shadow if death. full of fear, worry, anxiety, frustration, guilt, condemnation. Just the opposite of what the Word says we have when we're born-again of God's spirit.

Look, the first thing you do is love God. Secondly you love yourself. And thirdly you love your neighbor. Who's your neighbor? The bible says we have to be especially good to the household of what? Faith. That's your neighbor. So, stay put for awhile. Don't always think it's wonderful to love so-n-so up there whom I haven't seen. But if you can't love the people you have seen, how you going to love those birds that are out there that you've never seen? You see, that unity of that one body has to be there because of the greatness of that love of God in the renewed mind.

Boy, I want to tell you it's a wonderful Word of God. And it's a wonderful walk with God. In Colossians 3, beginning with verse 4. Then I go to verse 8, because verses 5, 6 and 7 are a parenthesis. They should be that in you're bible, but if they aren't, why don't you just mark it.

Colossians 3:4
When Christ, *who is* our life, shall appear, then shall ye also appear with him in glory.

Who is my life? Christ! Not the company that has an umbrella (in their logo). That insurance company is not my life. Who is my life? Now look, it's as simple as that. Do you believe God's Word, or don't you? You're never going to have that unity of that one body, that household of God, that family of faith, until we get the Word and say what the Word says. Christ is my life. O.K.! Then I don't get life from those other sources that the world would have me to believe that are capable of giving me everything; right? I get my life from whom? Christ! That's what it says, that's what it means.

"Shall appear, then shall ye also appear with him in glory." But now! But now! But now! But now! Verse 8, because he hasn't appeared yet. Right?

Colossians 3:8-10

8 But now ye also put off all these; anger, wrath, malice, blasphemy, filthy communication out of your mouth.

9 Lie not one to another, seeing that ye have put off the old man with his deeds;

10 and have put on the new *man,* which is renewed in knowledge after the image of him that created him:

Have put on the new man in our minds. And we have that unity, that one mind. Striving together for that gospel, with that one mind. Which is the mind of Christ.

Colossians 3:11-13

11 where there is neither Greek nor Jew, circumcision nor uncircumcision, Barbarian, Scythian, bond *nor* free: but Christ *is* all, and in all.

12 Put on therefore, as the elect of God, holy and beloved, bowels of mercies, kindness, humbleness of mind, meekness, longsuffering;

13 forbearing one another, and forgiving one another, if any man have a quarrel against any: even as Christ forgave you, so also *do* ye.

What if I don't want to forgive? The Lord said do it! It's not a question of whether I want to, it's the Word of God. And if I say I'm a Christian and I want to be in that household and stay in the unity of that one mind and that body I've got to do what the Word says. It's not a question of what I want, God say DO IT! Don't argue. "If any man have a quarrel against any: even as Christ forgave you, so also *do* ye." See how simple the Word is and how sharp it is? You can't have any difficulty with this if you make up your mind to go the way of the Word. But it's because we want to play the Word and the world against each other. And when we want to keep the people of the world happy, and keep God happy, we get in the soup. Can't do it, honey! It's either God's Word and we walk on it, or we go the way of the world.

> Colossians 3:14
> And above all these things *put on* charity, which is the bond of perfectness.

Charity is the love of God in the renewed mind in manifestation. Which is the bond, the cohesive, the binding element. It is that which binds together. The bond of perfectness.

> Colossians 3:15
> And let the peace of God rule in your hearts, to the which also ye are called in one body; and be ye thankful.

Maybe 1 Corinthians 13 speaks rather loudly. Or is it just words?

> 1 Corinthians 13:1-13
> [1] Though I speak with the tongues of men and of angels, and have not charity, I am become *as* sounding brass, or a tinkling cymbal.
>
> [2] And though I have *the gift of* prophecy, and understand all mysteries, and all knowledge; and

though I have all faith, so that I could remove mountains, and have not charity, I am nothing.

³ And though I bestow all my goods to feed *the poor*, and though I give my body to be burned, and have not charity, it profiteth me nothing.

⁴ Charity suffereth long, *and* is kind; charity envieth not; charity vaunteth not itself, is not puffed up,

⁵ doth not behave itself unseemly, seeketh not her own, is not easily provoked, thinketh no evil;

⁶ rejoiceth not in iniquity, but rejoiceth in the truth;

⁷ beareth all things, believeth all things, hopeth all things, endureth all things.

⁸ Charity never faileth: but whether *there be* prophecies, they shall fail; whether *there be* tongues, they shall cease; whether *there be* knowledge, it shall vanish away.

⁹ For we know in part, and we prophesy in part.

¹⁰ But when that which is perfect is come, then that which is in part shall be done away.

¹¹ When I was a child, I spake as a child, I understood as a child, I thought as a child: but when I became a man, I put away childish things.

¹² For now we see through a glass, darkly; but then face to face: now I know in part; but then shall I know even as also I am known.

[13] And now abideth faith, hope, charity, these three; but the greatest of these *is* charity

Talking about speaking in tongues. And have not the love of God in the renewed mind in manifestation. I; sure, I'm a Cristian, but I'm not in the household, in that one body; really walking with that one mind, the mind of Christ. Because I am become as a sounding brass or just a tinkling ole cymbal.

And though I have prophecy; you know I prophecy here on Sunday nights at the Way Headquarters. And understand all the mysteries that have been made known in God's Word, including the church, the body. And all knowledge, operate that wonderful word of knowledge. And though I have all believing, or faith, believing, the manifestation, you know. So, that I could even remove, you know, a what? Mountain! But if I do not have the love of God in the renewed mind in manifestation; I am what? Nothing! And nothing means nothing. You don't need a concordance to understand that, or a dictionary.

Sounding brass or a tingling cymbal. Kids today would say your just blowing hot air. Your all talk. 2nd verse says, I am nothing. Verse 3 is beautiful. And though I bestow all my income, all of my goods, to feed the poor. And even though I would give my body to be burned, I'd burned out my body, just bleed my heart out, for the teaching of God's Word, rightly divided. Couldn't be rightly divided if I didn't have the last part (of this verse). Have not the love of God in the renewed mind in manifestation, it profits me nothing.

The love of God in the renewed mind in manifestation suffereth long (verse 4). It's kind. The love of God in the renewed mind envieth not. The love of God in the renewed mind vaunteth not itself, it is not rash, or brash. It's not puffed up, it's not an ego trip. It does not behave itself unseemly (verse 5). Seeketh not her own. About everything in here the world does just the opposite, you know that! the world seeketh its own. It behaves unseemly. Just the opposite. That last part of verse 5 is a real heavy; thinketh no evil. That's the love of God in the renewed mind. That one body, that unity, that must be there if the Words to move. Thinketh no evil. Have you blown this one today?

Rejoiceth not in iniquity (verse 6). But rejoices, it gets real happy, in the truth. Beareth all things that the Word of God says you are to bear, else it is not renewed mind. Believeth all things that the Word of God says you believe. Hopeth all things that the Word of God says your to hope for. And endureth all things that the Word of God says you have to endure.

The love of God in the renewed mind never faileth (verse 8). But, weather there be prophecy, they're going to quit, fail. Speaking in tongues, what's going to happen to it? Cease. Word of Knowledge, what's going to happen to it? It's going to vanish away, it's going to fail too. For with all of the greatness of what God has given we still know in part only. And we prophecy in part.

But, and praise God, verse 10. When that which is perfect is come, and that's the return of the Lord Jesus Christ. When we shall be as he is, because, you know, we shall see him. Then, that which is in part will be done away with.

When I was a child, I spake as a child, I understood as a child, I thought as a child: but when I became a man, I put

65

away childish things. For now, right now, we see like through a glass, or in a mirror, darkly. But then, when Christ returns, face to face. Now I know in part, but then I will know even as also I am known.

And now, right now, abideth faith, hope, charity; which is the love of God in the renewed mind in manifestation. These three; but the greatest of these is the love of God in the renewed mind in manifestation. What a tremendous reality.

In 2 Corinthians, there's a record here in the 13th chapter that I'd just like to share with you before I close. Remember, the Corinthians were like the Philippians, they were in practical error, and God gave this Word to them of reproof and correction. To bring them back on the ball. And in this 13th chapter, after the whole record to the Corinthians had been given by God, the final word is, in verse 11.

> 1 Corinthians 13:11
> Finally, brethren, farewell. Be perfect, be of good comfort, be of one mind, live in peace; and the God of love and peace shall be with you.

Be of good comfort, be of one mind. **ONE MIND. ONE MIND.** Live in peace. And, doing that, the God of love and peace shall be with you. And unless we do that the God of love and peace cannot abide on the people, because the people have walked away from God. That's why He wrote them this great record, by divine revelation. That's why the Word of God is God breathed. Holy men of God spake as they were moved. And all scripture is profitable for right believing, for reproof and for correction. That we may be instructed in the perfect will of God. Be perfect! Have that same mind which was in Christ Jesus. And that mind of

Christ gets rid of fear, and worry, and anxiety, and frustration, and guilt, and condemnation, and criticism, and bitterness, and fault finding, back biting. All of that is gone when we walk by the revelation of His Word and just carry out the Word.

Well, ladies and gentlemen, if God so loved the He gave, what you and I have according to the word, in Christ Jesus. Can you and I do less than to love the brethren, and be especially good to the household of God, the household of faith? Not if we want to see the Word live.

Made in the USA
Monee, IL
11 April 2021